MW01043113

A is for ★ Alchemy

A Guide for the Little Conscious Creator

Written by: Esther Reese

Illustrated by: Bre'Anna Washington

A is for Alchemy

is dedicated to
Jaiana, Journei, Jamari, Jazzlyn, and JeMarcus, who have reminded me to heal my inner child, and to every child, young and old, who needs to remember their magic. -Esther Reese

Dear Adult Readers,

Thank you for exposing the child in your life to this book. These topics are not always discussed, but are becoming a huge part of our society as we collectively return to practices that remind us of the magic within.

A is for Alchemy is intended to build curiosity at a young age by encouraging youth to explore their own gifts, and as a result, grow into them more smoothly and securely with time.

Please use this book as a conversation starter and feel free to research topics that you're not familiar with. The learning process is to be enjoyed by everyone. Create consciously!

Love Always,
Esther Reese

A is for Alchemy

All avenues of alchemy are actualized by the atoms that make you aware. Alter from average to amazing. Transformation in alchemy is clear.

B is for Breathing

Become one with your breath to blast away bothersome thoughts and feelings. Spirit lives in the breath and is consciously used by the brightest of beings.

C is for Crystals

Crystals are compacted earth energy. Carry, collect, and charge them in the sun. When used to cleanse and attract, you'll have lots of fun!

D is for Dreams

You lie down at night to drift away. Anew world dances in your mind for you to learn and play.

E is for Elements

Each and every element has a different effect. Experiment with each to see where you naturally connect.

F is for Frequency

Feel free when you fill yourself with a high frequency. Fly above false fear by tuning in frequently.

G is for Growth

Give room to get bigger, faster, and smarter. Growing is an ongoing gift but without patience, it gets harder!

H is for Holistic

On Earth, natural law may be hard to remember. The whole being's mind, body, and soul must be considered.

Iis for Intuition

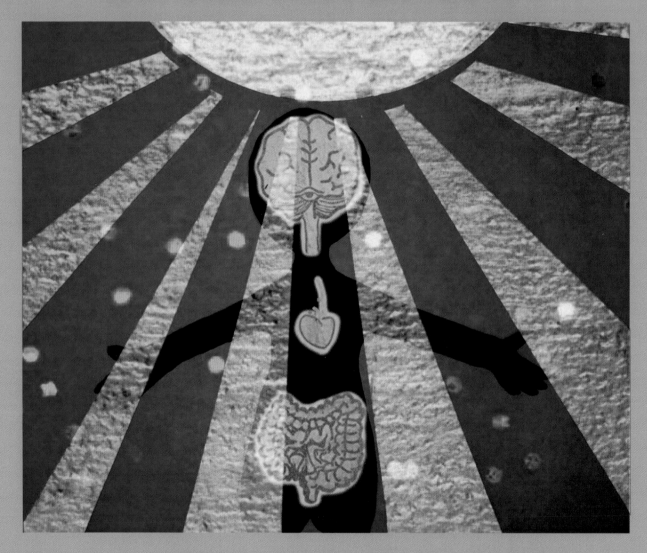

Is it hard for you to make a decision? The first idea is the right one, it's your inner-voice. Trust your intuition.

J is for Juju

Just juggle those joyous elements. What type of magic do you like to create? It's no secret that your gifts are heaven-sent.

K is for Karma

Karma is the cycle that keeps on coming. Every action creates a reaction. What you reap comes from what you're sowing.

L is for Love

Love is a long-lasting healing vibration.
Life is more fulfilling when love of self and
others is the motivation.

M is for Manifest

Make the most of your mission. Mark the world with meaningful miracles through focus and intention.

N is for Nature

Let nature be your nurse when you're not feeling nice. Tune in with your feet in the soil or stargaze at night.

O is for Offering

Open the opportunity for outstanding outcomes by offering what you can. What can you give up to originate your plan?

P is for Prayer

Put passion to your purpose with the use of your tongue. Speak to your Power and receive gifts, one by one.

Q is for Questions

Quit starving your knowledge by keeping quiet in the face of the unknown. Quality questions are a quick route home.

R is for Rest

Restore your vessel with rejuvenating rest. Receiving insight with a refreshed perspective keeps you at your best.

S is for Self

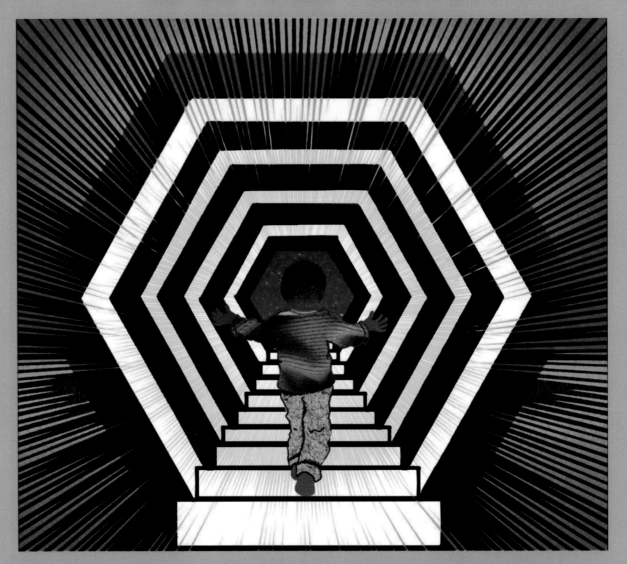

Self is your true nature, the soul, and the spirit. Stay in tune with yourself with love, trust, and respect to overcome all limits.

T is for Transcend

Trust that your time here is only a transit.
Transform your trials. This life is expansive.

U is for Unity

Create unison within you, then your family, and community. Cosmic union is the ultimate goal of unity.

V is for Vibration

Vibration is versatile. It is moods, feelings, and thoughts. Low vibes of fear, doubt, and sadness are not very helpful. Remain vigilant. Vibrate up!

W is for Wisdom

When we work towards incorporating the knowledge and understanding we've encountered, the wisdom from within overflows like a fountain.

X is for X-Chromosome

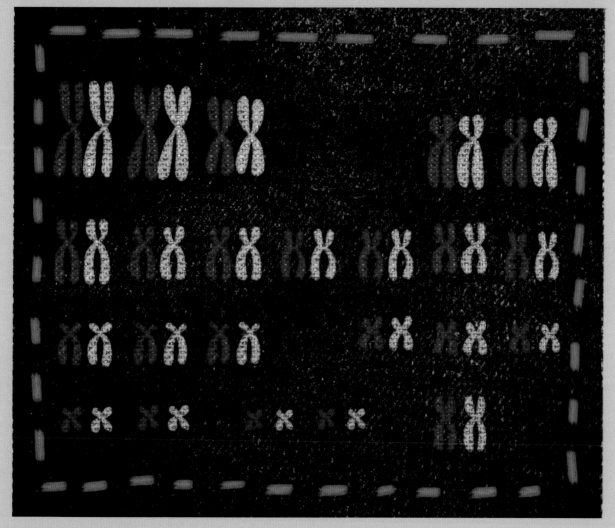

The excellence of our experience is encoded in our DNA. Genes and traits from our parents express themselves here in extraordinary ways.

Y is for Yoga

With yoga poses, you push past your limits yet start to feel yummy. Tune the mind, body, and spirit into one with deep stretches and breaths that begin in the tummy.

Z is for Zodiac

Zooming through the cosmos, the stars play and tell a zealous story. Use astrology to comprehend the patterns of life, plan events, and identify your times of glory.

I am an Alchemist.
My dreams are coming true.
I am loved.
I have the courage to be myself.
I trust in my abilities.
I am intelligent.
I listen to my inner wisdom.
Every problem has an answer.
I accept and love myself.
I learn from my mistakes.
Miracles happen to me.
I am grateful for my life.